The Alhambra
and the Generalife

TEXT

Ricardo Villa-Real

PHOTOGRAPHS

Javier Algarra - Miguel Sánchez - Ángel Sánchez.

Ediciones Miguel Sánchez

© **Ediciones Miguel Sánchez:** Marqués de Mondéjar, 44. Granada.

© **Photograph:** Javier Algarra and Ediciones Miguel Sánchez.

Text: Ricardo Villa-Real.

Translation: Karen Otto de García.

Updated revision of the translation: Carolina Román Fernández.

Design and Layout: Bitono (Paqui Robles).

Photosetting: Panalitos, S.L.

Printed by: Grefol, S.L., Móstoles (Madrid).

Paper: CREATOR SILK TORRAS PAPEL

ISBN: 84-7169-067-5

Depósito legal: GR-1061/2001

Printed in Spain

The very mention of the Alhambra is enough to evoke in many people's minds the spell of an historic past, teeming with life, and the charm of certain exotic legends that pique the imagination with this magic word. "Yet", as Angel Ganivet remarked, "there are some people who visit the Alhambra and believe they sense the lulling and allure of sensuality, but fail to sense the profound sadness that emanates from a deserted palace, forsaken by its inhabitants, imprisoned in the impalpable threads woven by the spirit of destruction, that invisible spider whose feet are dreams".

The *Alhambra* of Granada is a unique monumental complex, in which a number of exceptional circumstances are combined. One of them is its topography. Rising upon the hill of La Sabica it dominates the whole city, which is beheld and courted like a wife. That is the image which inspired the Arab poet Ibn Zamrak in the 14th century:

"Pause on the esplanade of La Sabika and gaze upon your surroundings.
"The city is a lady whose husband is the hill.
"She is clasped by the belt of the river,
"And flowers smile like jewels at her throat...
"La Sabika is a crown upon the brow of Granada,
"In which the stars yearn to be studded.
"And the Alhambra — God watch over it!
"Is a ruby at the crest of that crown".

From this hilltop location any tower or window, wall or archway easily affords the opportunity to reflect upon unparalleled scenery and panorama-upon harmony, sound and light.

The name *Alhambra* comes from an Arabic root which means "red" *(alqala hamrá,* red or crimson castle), perhaps due to the iron hue of the towers and of the walls that surround the entire hill of La Sabica, "which by starlight is silver, but by sunlight is transformed into gold," says an Arab poet. But

View of the Alhambra from the Albayzín.

"LA SABIKA IS A CROWN UPON THE BROW OF GRANADA..
AND THE ALHAMBRA —GOD WATCH OVER IT! IS A RUBY AT THE CREST OF THAT CROWN ".

IBN ZAMRAK.

The Albayzín from the walls of the fortress or Alcazaba.

3

Window at the Wine Gate.

*Latticework at the Court
of the Myrtles.*

Fountain at the Court of the Lions.

there is another, more poetic version, evoked by the Moslem annalists who speak of the construction of the Alhambra fortress "by the light of torches," the reflections of which gave the walls their particular coloration.

Created originally for military purposes, the Alhambra was an *alcazaba* (fortress), an *alcázar* (palace) and a small *medina* (city), all in one. This triple character helps to explain many distinctive features of the monument. Nor should we find strange the curious marriage, contrived by history itself, between Moslem art-so delicate and fragile here, with "poor substances converted into artistic substance" (Gómez Moreno)-and Christian art, robust and full of an emerging balance.

There is no reference to the Alhambra as a residence of kings until the 13th century, even though the fortress had existed since the 9th century. The first kings of Granada, the Zirites *(ziríes)*, had their castles and palaces on the hill of the Albayzín, and nothing remains of them save the memory. The Nasrites *(nasríes)* were probably the emirs who, commencing in 1238, built the Alhambra. The founder of the dynasty, Muhammad Al-Ahmar, began with the restoration of the old fortress. His work was completed by his son Muhammad II whose immediate successors continued with the repairs. The construction of the palaces (called *Casa Real Vieja,* "Old Royal House or Palace") dates back to the 14th century and is the work of two great kings: Yusuf I and Muhammad V. To the first we owe, among others, the *Cuarto de Comares* (Chamber of Comares), the *Puerta de la Justicia* (Gate of Justice), the Baths and some towers; his son, Muhammad V, completed the beautification of the palaces with the *Cuarto de los Leones* (Chamber of the Lions), as well as other rooms and fortifications.

The Alhambra became a Christian court in 1492, when the Catholic Monarchs (Ferdinand and Isabella) conquered the city of Granada. Later, various structures were built for prominent civilians and for military garrisons, in addition to a church and a Franciscan monastery. Emperor Charles V, who spent several months in Granada, began the construction of the palace which bears his name and made some alterations in the interior buildings. These measures were to cause interminable controversy, in which criticism has often been motivated by political considerations. The rest of the Austrian kings did not forget the monument and have left their light and discreet impressions on it.

But then, during the 18th century and part of the 19th, the Alhambra, neglected, was to see its salons converted into dungheaps and taverns, and occupied by thieves and beggars. "Thus bats defile abandoned castles, thus the reality of Spanish crime and mendicancy disenchant the illusion of this fairy palace of the Moor", says the aggressive Richard Ford. As the crowning blow, Napoleon's troops, masters of Granada from 1808 until 1812, were to convert the palaces into barracks, and, in retreat on September 17th, he mined the towers and blew up part of them. Two of them, the *Torre de Siete Suelos* (Tower of Seven Floors) and the *Torre del Agua* (Water Tower) are left in ruins.

And so the incredible neglect continued, until 1870 when the Alhambra was declared a national monument. Travelers and romantic artists of all countries had railed against those who scorned the most beautiful of their monuments. Since that date and up to our time, the Alhambra, protected, restored, cared for and even improved, has been preserved for the pleasure and admiration of all.

"Square and crimson towers
"Harlequins on stage
"Of a blue drama whose first performance
"Takes place over the green of the leaves.
"Alhambra, you who throws them out,
"Tighten the bow of the foliage
"Against a city of laces
"Which is walled on the ivy,
"Towers of wind and stone
"Flying over the landscape!

Rafael Guillén.

Setting of the different areas of the monument and the book chapters

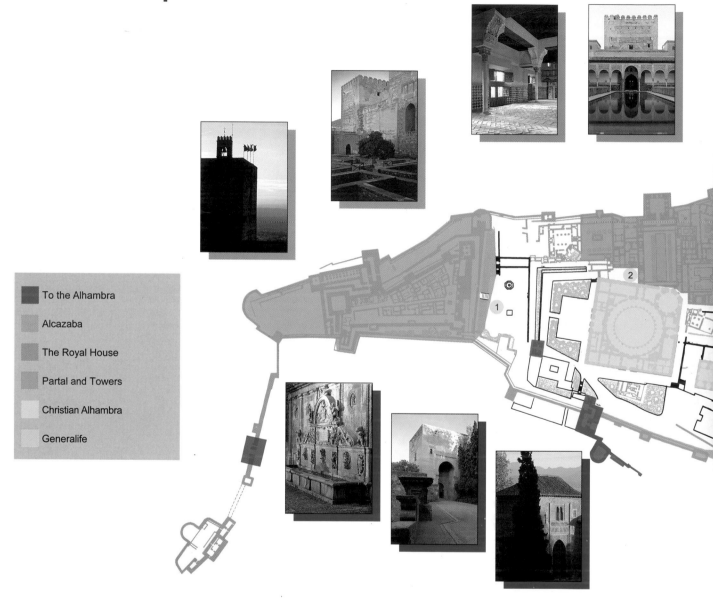

To the Alhambra

Alcazaba

The Royal House

Partal and Towers

Christian Alhambra

Generalife

RELEVANT INFORMATION:

With your ticket to the Alhambra you are entitled to visit the following areas:

1.- ALCAZABA: It is the area leading to the Puerta del Vino. The entrance is on the western side of the Court of the **Plaza de los Aljibes** (Square of the Cisterns) (number 1).

2.- PALACIOS: Access is allowed by the northern corner of the **Palace of Charles V.** (number 2).
For a detailed study on this area, please read sections The Royal House and Partal and Towers.
*Visitor must enter the palaces at the time specified on the ticket.

3.- GENERALIFE: Visitors can get into this area by different entrances. The main gate is next to the **tickets sale area** (number 3). Other ways to gain access are by the entrance next to the Parador de San Francisco, by walking across the area known as the **Secano** (number 4), or at the end of the promenade between the **Partal and Towers** (number 5).

···································· **Secano's area**
- - - - - - - - - - - - - - - - - - - **Partal and Towers' path**

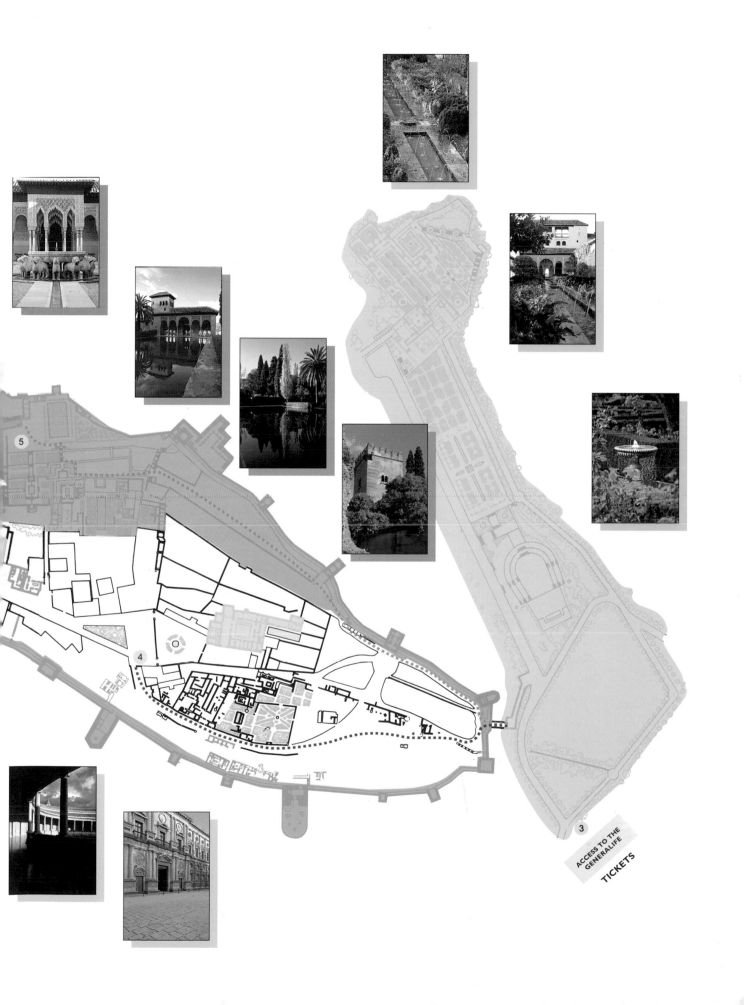

ACCESS TO THE GENERALIFE

TICKETS

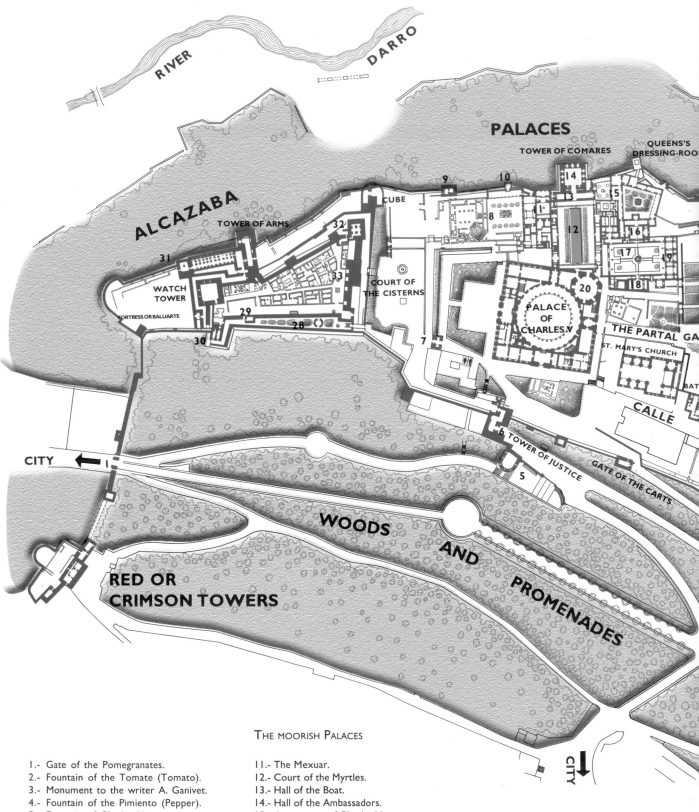

PLAN OF THE ALHAMBRA AND

RIVER DARRO

PALACES

TOWER OF COMARES

QUEEN'S DRESSING-ROOM

ALCAZABA

TOWER OF ARMS

CUBE

9

10

14

13

15

8

1

12

16

32

17

19

31

COURT OF THE CISTERNS

18

33

WATCH TOWER

20

PALACE OF CHARLES V

29

FORTRESS OR BALUARTE

28

7

THE PARTAL GA

ST. MARY'S CHURCH

30

CALLE

CITY

6 TOWER OF JUSTICE

GATE OF THE CARTS

5

RED OR CRIMSON TOWERS

WOODS AND PROMENADES

CITY

THE GENERALIFE

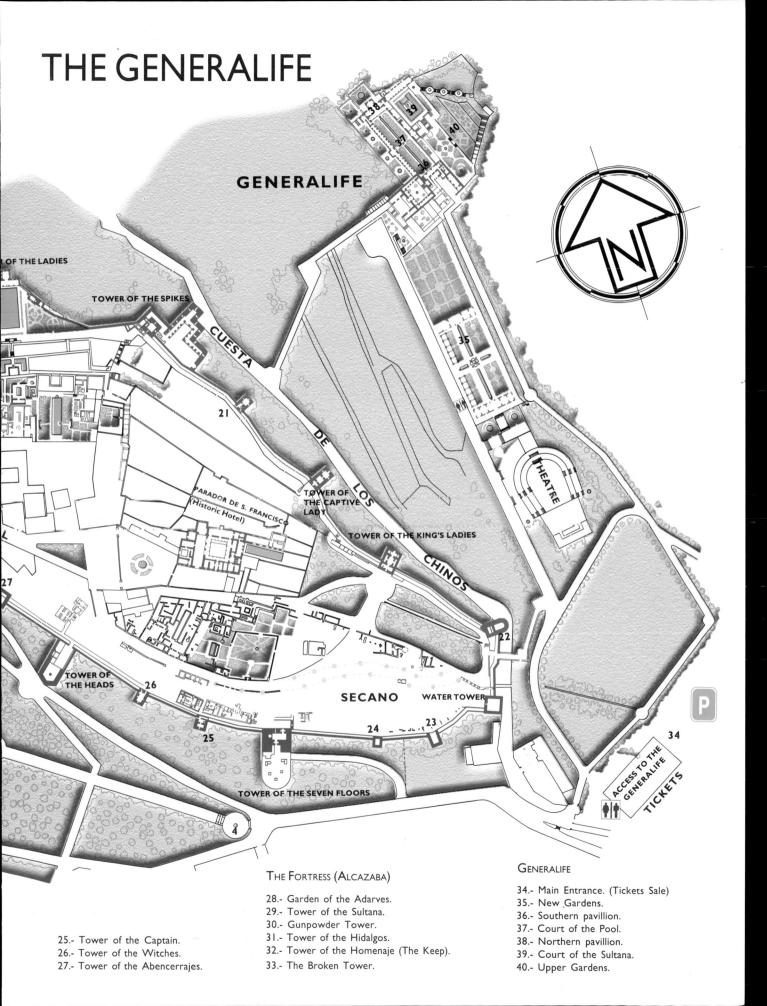

GENERALIFE

CUESTA DE LOS CHINOS

TOWER OF THE LADIES

TOWER OF THE SPIKES

21

PARADOR DE S. FRANCISCO
(Historic Hotel)

TOWER OF THE CAPTIVE LADY

TOWER OF THE KING'S LADIES

35

THEATRE

22

27

TOWER OF THE HEADS

26

25

SECANO

WATER TOWER

24   23

TOWER OF THE SEVEN FLOORS

P

34

ACCESS TO THE GENERALIFE

TICKETS

N

THE FORTRESS (ALCAZABA)

28.- Garden of the Adarves.
29.- Tower of the Sultana.
30.- Gunpowder Tower.
31.- Tower of the Hidalgos.
32.- Tower of the Homenaje (The Keep).
33.- The Broken Tower.

GENERALIFE

34.- Main Entrance. (Tickets Sale)
35.- New Gardens.
36.- Southern pavillion.
37.- Court of the Pool.
38.- Northern pavillion.
39.- Court of the Sultana.
40.- Upper Gardens.

25.- Tower of the Captain.
26.- Tower of the Witches.
27.- Tower of the Abencerrajes.

On Our Way to the Alhambra

Starting from Plaza Nueva, the road up the slope of the Cuesta de Gomérez ends at the **Puerta de las Granadas** (Gate of the Pomegranates), a sturdy and simple Renaissance structure which gives access to the Bosque (Woods) of the Alhambra, dating from the 18th and 19th centuries.

Once through the Gate of the Pomegranates, we have a choice of three roads. The one on the right goes to the Hill of Mauror, where the Torres Bermejas (Red or Crimson Towers) are. The middle road leads through the woods to the Generalife. Following the left-hand road, a steep slope takes us to the Pilar de Carlos V (Fountain of Charles V), a lovely Renaissance monument which boasts the coat-of-arms and emblems of the Emperor. The three grotesque faces apparently represent the three rivers of Granada (Genil, Darro and Beiro).

Behind the fountain is the **Puerta de la Justicia** (Gate of Justice), also called Puerta de la Ley (Gate of Law) and Puerta Judiciaria (Judicial Gate). Its tower is massive, and its surprising austerity reveals its military purpose. "Embattlemented tower, tinged with orange and gold, against a dark sky background" (T. Gautier). Two wide horseshoe arches form the entrance of the gate. On the outside is carved an outstretched hand, undoubtedly a talisman; perhaps the open fingers represent the five precepts of Koranic law. The second arch, smaller, has a key carved on its lintel, likely a symbol of power. Higher up, an inscription tells us that the gate was constructed by Yusuf I in 1348. And above the inscription there is an image of the Virgin and Child, of late Gothic style. Inside the gate a winding passage ends at a small, enclosed altarpiece. At its side a tablet, in complicated Gothic characters, speaks of the conquest of the city and the appointment of the Count of Tendilla as alcaide (governor) and captain. After leaving the gate's enclosure its rear façade should be observed. It is made of brick, but there are some very interesting remnants of the original tiles, of decorated enameled clay.

Next is a passageway with an unusual wall on the left, formed of Moslem funeral tablets. The passage leads to the **Plaza de los Aljibes** (Square of the Cisterns), handsome and expansive, with an Arab gateway before us, a Renaissance palace on the right, an exceptional panorama ahead, some high towers to our left...

At the very entrance of the esplanade is the **Puerta del Vino** (Wine Gate), which inspired Debussy, the man who wrote music about Spain without having visited it. "What the musician has wished to evoke in "La Porte du Vin" is the calm and luminous hour of the siesta in Granada", says Manuel de Falla. The gate presents a double façade of horseshoe arches. The western façade has a charming little double window. Above the portal runs a frieze; and on the central keystone appears, again, the magic key or talisman, indicating that this gate, now isolated, must have communicated in the past with the medina or city. The rear or western façade is very rich in painted and glazed enamelwork.

Western façade of the Gate of Wine.

Alcazaba

Located at the west of the Plaza de los Aljibes, the Alcazaba takes its name from the Arabic *al-qasba:* "fortress". It is the oldest part of the Alhambra, reconstructed upon the ruins of a castle in the 9th century. The most solid towers are those of *Homenaje* (Homage), and the *Quebrada* (Broken). The richest in its interior is the *Torre de las Armas* (Tower of Arms). All are surpassed in popularity and historical interest by the *Torre de la Vela* (Watch-Tower).

At the south of the Alcazaba is the delightful *Jardín de los Adarves* (Garden of the Wall Tops), also called *Jardín de los Poetas* (Garden of the Poets). From its battlements our gaze is drawn to the towers of the hill in the foreground. They are the *Torres Bermejas* (Red or Crimson Towers), the "castle of great worth" of a famous border ballad. Their bewitching name is evoked in the music of composers such as Albéniz or Joaquín Rodrigo.

The **Torre de la Vela** is the tallest tower of the walled enclosure and is also distinctive for its famous bell, rung on special festive occasions by those with the hope of getting the love of their lives. The landscape seen from here extends towards unlimited horizons and its silhouette is a significant symbol to the people of Granada.

The Watch Tower at dawn, the town hiding at its feet.

ABOVE: *Square of Arms, Towers of the Homenaje (Homage) and Quebrada (Broken).*
BELOW: *Garden of Wall Tops or Adarves, the garden of the poets.*

Tower of the Homage from the Square of Arms, at dawn.

View from the Alcazaba: the Tower of the Hens, the Tower of Comares and the Generalife.

The Royal House

T HIS ROYAL HOUSE *(Casa Real),* or PALACE is comprised of several palace groups, with a series of courts and structures surrounding them, which were born out of transitory or ornamental necessity. Since the 16th century these Nasrite *alcázares* (palaces) have been designated the *Casa Real Vieja* (Old Royal House) in order to distinguish them from the Christian building known as the *Casa Real Nueva* (New Royal House).

The Alhambra contains the three divisions usually found in a Moslem palace: the *Mexuar* or *Cuarto Dorado* (Gilded Chamber), a reception hall devoted to the public and to the administration of justice; the *Cuarto de Comares* (Chamber of Comares) or *Serrallo* (the Seraglio), official residence of the king or emir; and the *Cuarto de los Leones* (Chamber of the Lions) or *Harén* (Harem), intimate family apartments of the monarchs. These three branches are complemented by other dependencies also noteworthy.

ABOVE:

A column at the Hall of the Mexuar.

NEXT PAGES:

TOP LEFT:
Fret arabesque and socle at the Hall of the Mexuar.

RIGHT:
Hall of the Mexuar: "Come in and ask; do not be afraid of asking for justice, as this you will find."

Mexuar

A modest passageway, a door grating, a small courtyard. In the background, the portal of the *Mexuar,* section of the palace where the emir, either directly or through his cadí (magistrate), administered public justice two days a week. On entering, our first impression is one of disorder, as we notice that arabesques alternate with Christian motifs: a chapel choirloft, balustrades, railings, imperial escutcheons, nobiliary ensigns... No other hall of the Alhambra has suffered more modifications and alterations. In the center of the hall, the four marble columns no longer support the original dome, perhaps even balconies which have disappeared. It is also noteworthy to observe the beautiful stucco decoration on the walls.

From the windows on the left can be seen the **Jardín de Machuca** (Garden of Machuca, named after the architect) gallery or portico of festooned arches, with a garden of geometric outline and a graceful pool in the center. This was the original entrance for those who came from the quarters of the Almanzora and the Albayzín, across the bridges of the River Darro. At the rear of the hall of the *Mexuar,* a private *oratorio* or small mosque looks out upon the river valley. Its decoration, restored, is very lavish. Its *mihrab* (niche) indicates the east, towards which those who pray must face. It bears this significant inscription: "Be not among the negligent. Come and pray."

At the rear of the hall we pass into the **Patio del Mexuar** (Court of the Mexuar), with columns of unusual capitals. Behind the portico is the **Cuarto Dorado** (Gilded Chamber), today completely redone. The courtyard is small, and its function as anteroom is clearly seen. In the center is a marble basin, a copy of the original at the Garden of Daraxa, and opposite, our eyes meet the façade of the Chamber of Comares.

Court of the Mexuar and façade of the Chamber of Comares.

Detailed view of the façade of the Chamber of Comare

Cuarto de Comares (Chamber of Comares)

This was the official residence of the emir. Its splendid façade is of extraordinarily rich decoration and admirable composition. Its two doorways, of geometric symmetry, have frames of tile inlay (or glazed tiles); and above each are small double windows, panels and friezes with great ornamental richness. And covering the façade is a great projecting *alero* (cornice) of carved wood, with an inscription which begins: "My position is that of the crown, and my gateway is a crossroad. The East envies the West for my cause..."

Through the doorway on the left, along a winding passageway, we enter the **Patio de los Arrayanes** (Court of the Myrtles), also called *Patio de la Alberca* (Court of the Pool). This impressive courtyard, of rectangular shape in the purest tradition of Arabic architecture, measures 37 meters long by nearly 24 wide; and its pool serves as a mirror wherein the porticos and the Tower of Comares are reflected. Parallel to the water are two hedges of myrtle, or *arrayán*, from which the name comes. The south portico, adjoining the Palace of Charles V, is composed of seven arches of latticed fretwork.

Court of the Myrtles.
Northern portico and the Tower of Comares at the background.

"I HAVE THE FEELING OF BEING WITHIN A FANTASY, WITH SUCH A RYTHMICAL AND PURE
HARMONY THAT REMINDS ME OF THAT OF GREEK BUILDINGS." CAMILE MAUCLAIR, CRITIC,
ART HISTORIAN, FRENCH POET AND NOVELIST (1872-1945), TALKING ABOUT THIS COURT.

From this point the battlemented tower, the pool and the portico opposite form a chromatic and sensory union which, from all its elements, makes it the triumph of balance and the haven of peacefulness. "The rest is silence. There are no words to describe this *asylum pacis,* the most perfect and purest of all those which I have sought and found" (C. Mauclair).

The north portico has likewise seven arches above columns with stylized capitals of *mocárabes* (stalactites). And on the walls are pious supplications and poetic inscriptions. The ornamental characters in the Arabic script here are, in themselves, a decoration and an adornment. White cursive or kufic characters of verses from the Koran, pious maxims or *qasidas* (poems) are embossed upon darker backgrounds or upon tiled *zócalos* (lower wall portions).

The pointed arch in the center, with spandrels showing vegetation motifs and crowned by small latticed windows of plaster, is the entry to the **Sala de la Barca** (Hall of the Boat), which may owe its name either to the wooden roofing like a boat's keel, or more likely to the Arabic word *baraka* (greeting, blessing) which appears with profusion in the engraved inscriptions on the walls. In the jambs of the arch are some recesses of fine marble, faced within with ceramic, which were designed for flower vessels or lamp lights. The constant ornamental motif in the plaster covering of the walls is the escutcheon of the Nasrites, with the motto, "Only God is victorious." It seems clear that the function of this room was as antechamber of the adjoining **Salón de Embajadores** (Salon of the Ambassadors), which occupies the interior of the Tower of Comares. The tower measures 45 meters high and is a masterpiece of Yusuf I. The name is derived from the Arabic *qamaryya* (in Spanish, *comarías),* the colored glass windows that existed in the nine alcoves or open galleries of the hall. We can imagine the royal canopied throne on the balcony or recess in the center, facing the Court of the Myrtles. In this majestic hall, the dome is a masterpiece of Moslem carpentry, in dark cedar wood; the great frieze of *mocárabes* (stalactites) and the arabesques of the walls are marvels of stylization. In this hall Granada's fate was sealed when Boabdil and his Grand Council decided to surrender to the Catholic Monarchs, Ferdinand and Isabella.

View of the Hall of Ambassadors from the Hall of the Boat.
It was the centre of political talks in the moslem Granada.
During its glorious past the walls were covered with
polychromatic plasterwork.

ABOVE: *Ceiling at the Hall of Ambassadors. Masterpiece of the Moslem carpentry.*
RIGHT: *Inside the Hall, the mysterious brightness helps create that esoteric majesty of the royal throne so common among the Moslems.*

Cuarto de los Leones (Chamber of the Lions).

This third branch of the Alhambra palace has, like the two previous sections, a central courtyard surrounded by structures. It is the work of Muhammad V and illustrates the most beautiful possibilities of Granada Moslem art. Throughout this chamber a subtle air of femininity and daintiness is sensed in keeping with the function of these private apartments, devoted to the placid enjoyment of home and family life.

Above:
Fountain of the Lions and
East pavillion.

Right:
General view of the Court
of the Lions from the
Western gallery.

The **Patio de los Leones** (Court of the Lions) is characterized by its profound originality; and, in it, East and West merge harmoniously. It has been compared to a grove of 124 palmtrees, most with double columns, around the oasis of the central fountain with its twelve lions. But the slender *templetes* (niches) of triple arches make us think also of the cloister of a medieval monastery. It is the triumph of rhythm and symmetry.

THE COURT REMINDS OF A CLOISTER. IT IS PERHAPS A CHRISTIAN REMINISCENCE OF THE LINKS BETWEEN MUHAMMAD V WHO BUILT THIS COURT, AND HIS CHRISTIAN ALLY, PEDRO I.

ABOVE: *Detail of the basin and lions..." The lack of life refrains their fury."*
RIGHT: *Detail of the columns at the Court.* NEXT PAGE: *North-east corner of the Court.*

The twelve-sided marble **fountain** rests upon the backs of the lions. Water, so essential as a decorative element, acquires here an exceptional importance. The liquid ascends and spills from the basin. –which has been compared with the "sea of bronze" of Solomon's Temple– to the mouths of the lions, from which it is distributed throughout the courtyard. A lovely *qasida* (ode) by Ibn Zamrak circles the rim of the basin.

Four large halls border the courtyard. The first, entering from the Court of the Myrtles, is the **Sala de los Mocárabes** (Hall of Stalactites) whose name is perhaps derived from the three stalactite arches which form the entrance to the Court of the Lions. Part of the ceiling was laid in the 18th century; and today the result, save for the original walls, is coarse and incongruous.

To the south is the **Sala de Abencerrajes** (Hall of the Abencerrajes), famous in legend. Its gateway, decorated with *lazo* (ornamental knots), is the original. Light penetrates the hall through 16 graceful, little fretwork windows, opening in the extremely beautiful starry dome. The light is soft and vertical. The square hall has alcoves at either end. In the center is the famous fountain where, according to tradition, the nobles of the illustrious line of Abencerrajes were beheaded. Someone tries to convince us that the rust-colored stains on the marble are from the blood of those unhappy victims, still visible after centuries. And it is useless to try to prove they are only iron oxide... No, it is not easy in the Alhambra to destroy the fantasies of the imagination.

On the east side of the courtyard is the **Sala de los Reyes** (Hall of the Kings), called also *Sala de la Justicia* (Hall of Justice); odd and unusual, it resembles a theatrical set, divided in three sections which correspond to three lovely porticos, separated by double arches of *mocárabes* (stalactites), each based on a fretwork rhombus. The name of the hall is given by the picture on the vault or central dome, which apparently depicts ten Nasrite kings. These portrayals, as well as those in the other two adjacent alcoves, have been executed according to a miniatured technique of illumination. They represent fantastic and conventional scenes. Much debated and studied by experts, some Christian influence is clear in this corner of the Arab *alcázar* (palace).

North of the Court of the Lions is the **Sala de las Dos Hermanas,** (Hall of the Two Sisters), so called because of the two large marble flagstones flanking the central fountain and spout. The dome of *mocárabes* (stalactites) is admirable, and so is the treatment of light in this hall: the effect is that of richness, luminosity, enchantment. The decoration is based on *alicatados* (ceramic tile in-lay along the lower portion of the walls) and *atauriques* (stylized decoration with vegetation motif). A *qasida* (poem) by Ibn Zamrak, the poet who illustrated the walls of the Alhambra, runs along the tiled *zócalo* (lower wall portion). The adjoining hall is the **Sala de los Ajimeces** (arched windows with central pillars) with two balconies overlooking the Garden of Daraxa.

ABOVE: *Hall of the Abencerrajes.*
RIGHT: *Dome of the Hall of the Abencerrajes.*

ABOVE: *Hall of the Two Sisters.*
RIGHT: *Hall of the Kings.*

ABOVE: *Court of Daraxa.*
RIGHT: *Lookout of Daraxa.*

The bath: intimate and mysterious. A sanctuary and a place for enjoyment,
where the purifying water prepares the faithful to their prayers.
"Come in the name of god into the best house, a place of purity,
a place for reflexion".
Ibn-al-Ŷayyab.

Above:
Big tank at the Hall of Immersions.

Right:
Hall of Exudation.

Between these two balconies is the **Mirador de Daraxa** (Lookout of Daraxa), dressing-room and bedroom of the Sultana. It is a delightful retreat in this secluded section of the palace in the style of bay window or mirador. (A more popular name is *Lindaraja,* corruption of *Daraxa,* which means "house of the Sultana"). "And she directs the charger of her glance toward that landscape where the breeze frolics," says an inscription; for, formerly, before the Reconquest when the buildings now opposite were constructed, this room looked out over the Albayzín and the neighboring mountains. The tiled *zócalo* (lower wall) is extraordinary-perhaps the most complex, rhythmical and subtle in all the Alhambra, and surely the one with the most diminutive pieces. The windows are low, in keeping with the Moslem custom of reclining on the floor upon cushions and ottomans.

Through a plain hall adjoining the Hall of the Two Sisters we come to other sections of the palace. A suite of deserted rooms, *Habitaciones del Emperador* (the Emperor's Apartments), is situated above the Garden of Daraxa. Three of these rooms were occupied by Washington Irving, and in them he wrote his *Tales of the Alhambra.* The last hall gives access to the **Peinador de la Reina** (Queen's Dressing-room), also called the *Tocador* (Boudoir). An open gallery and an airy little tower, it was once designed as the residence of the Empress Isabel and later of Isabel of Parma, Philip V's wife. It is a *mirador* (lookout) and commands exceptional panoramas. Some restored frescoes portray scenes of Charles V's expedition to La Goleta.

Passing through the **Patio de los Cipreses** (Court of the Cypresses), unusual and unique, we come to the **Baños Reales** (Royal Baths), which may be closed to the public. The importance for Moslems of the bath is well known, as is its ceremonial and even sacred character.

These baths of the Alhambra are very complete and are related in their structure to the Roman bath. The first hall we enter is the *Sala del Reposo* (Hall of Repose) or *Sala de las Camas* (Hall of the Beds), which is actually the final resting place after a bath which would have taken place in the other rooms. It would have started in the *Sala de Immersión* (Hall of Immersion) with its marble tanks for cold and hot water, perfumed; and then it would have continued in the *Sala de Exudación* (Hall of Exudation), the famous Turkish bath, ending up in the *Sala del Reposo* or Hall of Repose. This last hall, which has been restored, is charming, with its four marble columns and its *alicatados* (tile in-lay), and three twin arches on the sides. The story above has four galleries from which, according to popular fancy, blind musicians interpreted sensuous melodies...

Next to the Baths is the **Jardín de Daraxa** (Garden-Court of Daraxa), or *Lindaraja*-not Moslem but Christian, and quite romantic. The original Arab fountain bears a song of praise inscribed on its rim. Off to one side of this garden are the cellars and the **Sala de los Secretos** (Hall of Secrets), delight of children of all ages because of its peculiar resonant qualities.

GALLERY BUILT DURING THE CHRISTIAN TIME, WITH WONDERFUL VIEWS TO THE ALBAYZIN, SACROMONTE AND DARRO VALLEY.

ABOVE:
The gallery and airy little tower at the Queen's Dressing-room.

BELOW:
Gallery and Tower of Comares.

Partal and Towers

The **Partal** (from the Arabic word for *portico*-lobby, piazza) is a group of recent gardens, graded in terraces. All around are the **Towers**. Cited in order they are: *Torre de las Damas* (Ladies), the small Oratory, *Torre de los Picos* (Spikes), *Torre del Cadi* (Magistrate) which the townspeople call *Torre del Candil* (Oil Lamp), *Torre de la Cautiva* (Captive Lady), *Torre de las Infantas* (King's Daughters), *Cabo de la Carrera* (End of the Track), *Torre del Agua* (Water Tower), *Torre de los Siete Suelos* (Seven Floors), *Torre del Capitán* (Captain), *Torre de la Bruja* (Witch)... until we reach the *Puerta de la Justicia* (Gate of Justice). Some of the towers have been reconstructed in our time. The Tower of the Ladies is an open portico, of five arches, with a large mirror-like pool. The Oratory (or little tower of the *mihrab,* «shrine») is elegant and has an irregular interior. The Tower of Spikes presents an unusual silhouette, as its brick merlons terminate in a pyramidical shape. It may be a Christian work.

Oratory at the Partal, seen from the portico at the Tower of the Ladies.

If the Tower of the Cadí has little to offer, the next two towers are most interesting. The Tower of the Captive Lady is the source of numerous legends connected with Isabel of Solís, concubine of Muley Abul Hassan. Its interior is richly decorated. The Tower of the Infantas is exquisitely feminine and coquettish, with its little central courtyard and waterspout and its graceful upper story or gallery. Unfortunately, we cannot always get into the towers, as the entrance may not be open to the public.

ABOVE: *Pool and gardens at the Partal.*
LEFT: *Pool at the Partal and Tower of the Ladies.*

Motifs at the façade of the Tower of the Captive Lady and Tower of the King´s Daughters

Sight across the Tower of the Captive Lady.

Tower of the Spikes seen from the Slope of Peebles.

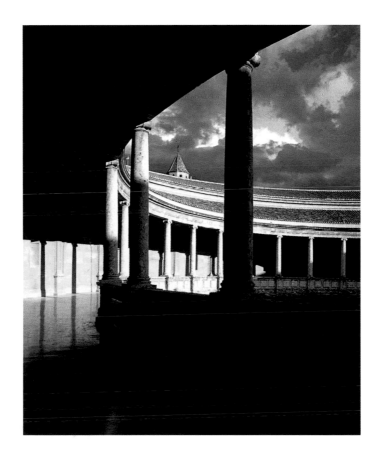

Christian Alhambra

W e have noted in passing some Christian influences in the towers and palaces. But within the Alhambra enclosure there are also monuments which are exclusively Western. For example, in the **Jardines de los Mártires** (Gardens of the Martyrs) there was once a monastery of the Carmelite order of which St. John of the Cross was prior.

The Church of St. Mary of the Alhambra was built upon the site where the royal mosque of the Alhambra formerly stood. The **Monastery of St. Francis** (today a government *parador,* or historical hotel) was erected upon an Arab palace, and has the additional merit and sentimental value of having housed the temporary sepulchre of the Catholic Monarchs-Ferdinand and Isabella-until their transfer to the *Capilla Real* (Royal Chapel) of Granada.

Upper Gallery at the Palace of Charles V. The contrast between the form of a square on the outside and a circular courtyard inside the building makes it a unique piece of architecture.

Palace of Charles V

Among all these Christian buildings the *Palacio de Carlos V* (Palace of Charles V) stands out. Called the *Casa Real Nueva* (New Royal House, or Palace), it

was commissioned by the Emperor in an endeavor to emulate the Palace of the defeated Moslems-and also to provide for himself a habitable residence. Although it may seem paradoxical, the building attains its full artistic justification and its validity precisely here, where the contrast is most violent. For we have passed brusquely from the fragile world-sensory, ethereal nuances of the Moslems, to the vigorous and forceful world, the triumph of order and balance.

Construction of the palace was begun in 1527 under the direction of Pedro Machuca, who had studied with Michelangelo in Italy. Subjected to a long series of interruptions, it is still unfinished. Its salons have been modernized, and the roofs of its upper gallery have been covered.

Today its most noble function is as headquarters for two museum: The Museum of the Alhambra and The Museum of Fine Arts. It also serves as the setting for concerts of the International Festival of Music and Dance.

The palace is a building in the form of a square and comprised of two main parts: the first, in Tuscan style; and the second with Ionic pilasters, a great circular courtyard and a ring-shaped vault. Of its four façades in *almohadillado* (that is, the part of the wall with squared masonry) only two are finished in their decoration: the southern and the western. The most important is the western façade, with three gateways, *frontón* (pediment) and cornice, magnificent medallions showing horsemen, and bas-reliefs with military insignia, as well as emblems and mythological figures. Great bronze rings hang from lion or eagle heads. The Doric columns of the lower part are of *pudinga* granite. The second part of the gallery rests upon Ionic columns.

The impression given by the Palace of Charles V-a very important landmark of Renaissance art, is one of sobriety, of solidity and of classical elegance.

LEFT:

Circular courtyard and double gallery at the Palace of Charles V.

ABOVE:

Southern façade of the Palace.

Western façade of the Palace of Charles V.

The Generalife

"Generalife, garden that had no match", says a celebrated border ballad. And someone has called it "the noblest and most exalted of all gardens". The Alhambra is complemented by the Generalife, a complex of gardens and white buildings, resting on and seemingly clinging to the hillside facing the palaces. Long ago there was a royal *almunia* (garden) here, planned as a playground for the Nasrite emirs. Gentle, tamed Nature with ineffable charm, the Generalife is a combination of trees and flowers, formal gardens, and *miradores* and galleries. It inspired Manuel de Falla's nocturne, "In the Generalife" of his symphonic poem, "Nights in the Gardens of Spain". And this music, in its sensory and direct impressionism, renders better than poetry or painting the pleasure of the silence, and of the sounds of the water, and of the perfumes of the vegetation.

Court at the Generalife leading to the stairs which end in the Court of the Long Pond.

View from the New Gardens of the Generalife

SUNRISE IN THE ALHAMBRA! THE ALBAYZÍN WAKES UP AND THE TOWERS LIGHT UP WITH THE FIRST RAYS OF THE DAY.

ABOVE: *Central pool at the New Gardens.*
RIGHT: *Central Fountain at the Court of the Long Pond.*

The word *Generalife* has been translated as "garden of paradise," "orchard" or "garden of feasts," "house of delights," etc. The most correct interpretation is that of "garden of the architect" *(Gennat alarif, alarife* is "builder"). After the city was conquered, the Generalife was granted by the Catholic Monarchs to the Granada Venegas family. The last private owner was the Marquis of Campotéjar. And since 1921 it has been the property of the State.

There are different ways to gain access to the gardens: by the main door, next to the ticket office; by a gate next to the *Parador de San Francisco* and walking through the secano, at the end of the route between the *Partal and Towers.*

Across the main gate we find a pathway surrounded by cypresses which splits into two directions: on the right, cypresses embrace all the way, whereas the main way leads to the **New Gardens.**

The New Gardens are embelished with rose bushes; pergolas and geometry – always with the poem of the water. These gardens, although modern, are very much in the Granada style and delightful to see and enjoy. At the far end we see a large open-air stage where every year the ballet and theatre programs of the International Festival of Music and Dance are performed.

The landscape is crowned by the sight of the Alhambra and the Albayzín on the left and northern side. The end of this promenade leads to two old patios: First, the **Patio del Polo** and then, a second pation embelished with orange trees and a central fountain which acts as a antechamber to the **Patio de la Acequia** (Court of the Long Pond).

This most celebrated spot, heart and soul of the palace grounds, is rectangular and has porticoed pavillions on its north and south sides, On the western side a gallery of 18 arches frames lovely and unique views of the Alhambra and the city. Through the courtyard splashes the famous long channel of waterspouts, surrounded by hedges of myrtle and of roses, amid cypresses and orange trees. It is the poem of the water-humble, chaste and lovely...

LEFT: *Court of the Long Pond seen from the lookout at the southern portico.*

NEXT PAGES:

UPPER/LEFT: *Generalife and Sierra Nevada.*
LOWER/LEFT: *Court of the Long Pond, northern portico.*
RIGHT: *Court of the Long Pond, southern portico.*

…»The waters speak, and they weep
"Beneath the white oleanders;
"Beneath the rose oleanders,
"The waters weep, and they sing,
"For the myrtle in bloom,
"Above the opaque waters.
"Madness of singing and crying,
"of the souls, of the tears!"…

ABOVE:
Court of the Cypresses or of the Sultana.
BELOW:
Stairs with cascading waterfalls.

Of the two porticoes, the most interesting one is the northern portico, called the **Mirador** *(lookout)* **of the Generalife.** It has five arches in front, slender and stylized, and three behind, of marble, with stalactite capitals. The five little overhead windows are exquisite, and so is the stucco grille-work, or lattice. In the square compartment of the three arches there is an inscription which furnishes us with precise data about the construction (the year 1319, during the reign of the Nasrite emir of Granada, Abul Walid Ismail). The arcade or portico is in front of a hall from which we obtain an excellent view of the Albayzín and the Sacromonte.

Through the north portico we pass to the **Patio de los Cipreses** (Court of the Cypresses), also called **Patio de la Sultana,** with a pool in the center. The distribution of the small ponds is charming, with their frames of oleander and myrtle, and their spouts in such profusion.

Against the edge of the rampart wall are two old cypresses. In the decayed trunk of one of them-so goes the tradition-the king (perhaps Muley Abul Hassan) surprised the sultana, his wife, with an Abencerraje nobleman, thus provoking the massacre of the entire clan. (Delightful fable by that great weaver of fables, Ginés Pérez de Hita).

A little stone step lifts us to the Upper Gardens, which were once olive groves, and today boast a handsome esplanade and modern gardens. Here is the unusual stairway with its cascading waterfalls, described by Navagiero as early as the 16th century, as hollow channels down which the water runs. The stairway leads to a modern, uninteresting edifice of several stories. At the end of the esplanade in the Upper Gardens is the entrance to the upper part of the southern portico in the Court of the Long Pond, which we can now view from a different perspective.

We start our way out by walking along the **Paseo de las Adelfas** (rose-bay, oleander, rhododendron) with a vault of flowers. The poet Juan Ramón Jiménez, "heart seized, as if wounded then convalescent," with "the light and the water that form in my depths the most prodigious labyrinths-low heavens, delirious generalifes," sings thus:

> ... *"The waters speak, and they weep*
> *"Beneath the white oleanders;*
> *"Beneath the rose oleanders,*
> *"The waters weep, and they sing...*

This promenade ends in the **Paseo de los Cipreses** (Promenade of the Cypresses).

Contrasting strongly with the fertility of the Generalife is the harsh landscape of the mountain which shelters it. Young pines and scrawny olive trees struggle in an ochre earth which is unacquainted with water. It is the *Cerro del Sol* (Peak of the Sun) or *Colina de Santa Elena* (St. Helen's Hill). Ruins and lovely recollections abound on the slopes of this mountain. Among them is the **Silla del Moro** (the Moor's Seat), very near the Generalife and on a higher elevation. Here is an ideal spot for contemplating the Alhambra, the valley of the Darro, the Generalife, the Albayzín and part of the city – and the ideal time of day is in the late afternoon; for...

Foutain at the Generalife, within the New Garden.

"How hard it is for the daylight
"To take its leave of Granada!
"It entangles itself in the cypress
"Or hides beneath the water."

Federico García Lorca.

ABOVE: *Fountains at the Generalife*   RIGHT: *Fountain at the Court of the Long Pond*

"The water takes your dream,
"asleep you are taken by the water,
"the water that I do not drink.
"Asleep over the silence
"Of the song that I do not sing
"*Because I sing it to myself*

Index
of photographs

 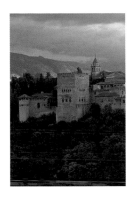 

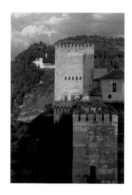

25.- Page. 25.
Court of the Myrtles from the Hall of the Boat.
PHOTOGRAPH BY A. SÁNCHEZ.

26.- Pages. 26 and 27.
General view of the Court of the Myrtles.
PHOTOGRAPH BY J. ALGARRA.

27.- Page. 29.
Hall of Embassadors from the Hall of the Boat.
Photograph by J. Algarra.

28.- Page. 30.
Dome at the Hall of Ambassadors.
Photograph by J. Algarra.

29.- Page. 31.
Hall of the Ambassadors.
PHOTOGRAPH BY J. ALGARRA.

30.- Page. 32.
Fountain of the Lions and East pavillion.
PHOTOGRAPH BY A. SÁNCHEZ.

31.- Page. 33.
General view of the Court of the Lions from the Western gallery.
PHOTOGRAPH BY J. ALGARRA.

32.- Pages. 34 and 35.
Perspective of the Court of the Lions.
PHOTOGRAPH BY J. ALGARRA.

33.- Page. 36.
Detail of basin and lions.
PHOTOGRAPH BY A. SÁNCHEZ.

34.- Page. 37.
Detail of the columns at the Court of the Lions.
PHOTOGRAPH BY M. SÁNCHEZ.

35.- Page. 39.
North-east corner of the Court.
PHOTOGRAPH BY J. ALGARRA.

36.- Page. 40.
Hall of the Abencerrajes.
PHOTOGRAPH BY M. SÁNCHEZ.

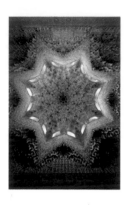

61.- Page. 66.
The Generalife and Sierra Nevada.
PHOTOGRAPH BY M. SÁNCHEZ.

62.- Page. 66.
Court of the Long Pond, northern portico.
PHOTOGRAPH BY A. SÁNCHEZ.

63.- Page. 67.
Court of the Long Pond, southern portico.
PHOTOGRAPH BY J. ALGARRA.

64.- Page. 68.
Court of the Cypresses.
PHOTOGRAPH BY A. SÁNCHEZ.

65.- Page. 68.
Stairs with cascading waterfalls.
PHOTOGRAPH BY A. SÁNCHEZ.

66.- Page. 69.
Foutain at the Generalife, within the New Garden.
PHOTOGRAPH BY J. ALGARRA.

67.- Page. 70.
Fountains at the Generalife.
PHOTOGRAPH BY A. SÁNCHEZ.

68.- Page. 71.
Fountain at the Court of the Long Pond.
PHOTOGRAPH BY A. SÁNCHEZ.